Cheerleading

by Sara Green

BELLWETHER MEDIA • MINNEAPOLIS, MN

Note to Librarians, Teachers, and Parents:

Blastoff! Readers are carefully developed by literacy experts and combine standards-based content with developmentally appropriate text.

Level 1 provides the most support through repetition of high-frequency words, light text, predictable sentence patterns, and strong visual support.

Level 2 offers early readers a bit more challenge through varied simple sentences, increased text load, and less repetition of high-frequency words.

Level 3 advances early-fluent readers toward fluency through increased text and concept load, less reliance on visuals, longer sentences, and more literary language.

Level 4 builds reading stamina by providing more text per page, increased use of punctuation, greater variation in sentence patterns, and increasingly challenging vocabulary.

Level 5 encourages children to move from "learning to read" to "reading to learn" by providing even more text, varied writing styles, and less familiar topics.

Whichever book is right for your reader, Blastoff! Readers are the perfect books to build confidence and encourage a love of reading that will last a lifetime!

This edition first published in 2011 by Bellwether Media, Inc.

No part of this publication may be reproduced in whole or in part without written permission of the publisher. For information regarding permission, write to Bellwether Media, Inc., Attention: Permissions Department, 5357 Penn Avenue South, Minneapolis, MN 55419.

Library of Congress Cataloging-in-Publication Data
Green, Sara, 1964–
 Cheerleading / by Sara Green.
  p. cm. – (Blastoff! readers: my first sports)
 Includes bibliographical references and index.
 Summary: "Simple text and full-color photographs introduce beginning readers to the sport of cheerleading. Developed by literacy experts for students in grades two through five"–Provided by publisher.
 ISBN 978-1-60014-568-1 (hardcover : alk. paper)
 1. Cheerleading–Juvenile literature. I. Title.
LB3635.G74 2010
791.6'4–dc22   2010035268

Printed in the United States of America, North Mankato, MN.
010111   1176

Contents

What Is Cheerleading?

Do you like to cheer your classmates on when they play sports? Do you like to perform in front of crowds? If so, you might make a great cheerleader!

Cheerleaders dance, **tumble**, and cheer to support sports teams. They also raise school spirit at **pep rallies**.

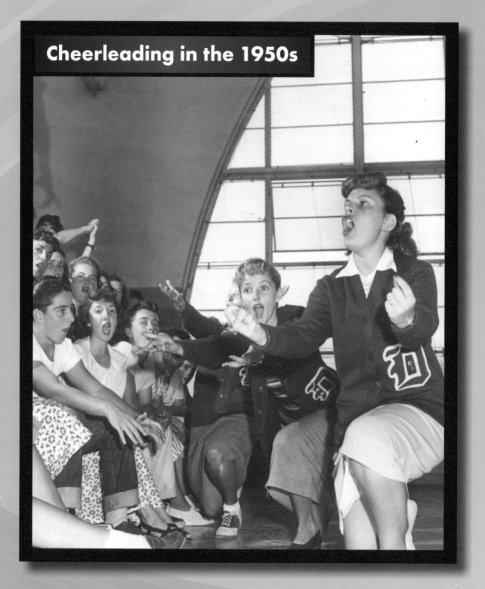

Cheerleading in the 1950s

Cheerleading began in 1898. At a University of Minnesota football game, student Johnny Campbell led an excited crowd in cheers. Soon, many universities had cheerleading **squads**.

At first, only men could be cheerleaders. Women started cheering in 1923. Today, there are millions of cheerleaders all over the world!

fun fact

Although cheerleading squads can include both females and males, 95 out of every 100 cheerleaders are female.

Cheerleading Equipment

pom-poms

! fun fact

The first pom-poms were made of crepe paper. When cheerleaders shook these pom-poms, strands of paper would fly into the air.

Cheerleaders use a variety of equipment when they cheer. Members of a squad wear athletic shoes and matching uniforms.

They shake colorful **pom-poms**. Some even yell into **megaphones** to raise their voices over noisy crowds.

megaphone

Stunts and Jumps

Cheerleaders must be strong and **flexible** to perform **stunts**. They must be able to climb, tumble, jump, and throw. Every member of a squad is important during a stunt.

Bases stand on the ground, and **flyers** stand on top of them. The bases throw the flyers into the air. The flyers do spins or flips, and the bases catch them when they land. **Spotters** are ready to help bases catch the flyers if they fall.

flyers

bases

spotters

Cheerleaders also perform many kinds of jumps. One popular jump is the **toe touch**. Cheerleaders jump and kick their legs out to the sides.

They reach toward their toes with their hands. With practice, cheerleaders can increase the heights of their jumps. Many cheerleaders can do splits high in the air!

Kinds of Cheerleading

All-star cheerleading and school cheerleading are the most popular kinds of cheerleading today. All-star cheerleading is also called competitive cheerleading.

School cheerleaders cheer at school sporting events, such as football and basketball games. They **rally** the crowds and the sports teams. Most middle schools, high schools, and colleges have cheerleading squads.

In all-star cheerleading, squads compete against each other. Cheerleaders join squads based on their ages and skill levels.

The squads do **routines** set to music. Judges give squads points for how well they tumble, jump, and cheer. They also give points for creativity and **good sportsmanship**.

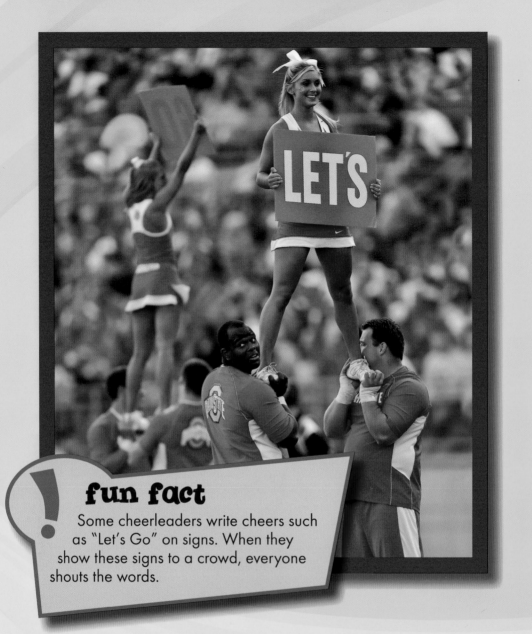

The most talented high school and all-star cheerleaders can become college cheerleaders. College cheerleaders often cheer in front of thousands of sports fans!

They do very complex stunts. One is called the twisting basket toss. A flyer twists high in the air before landing in the arms of a few bases.

Many high school and college cheerleading squads attend national cheerleading competitions. Cheerleaders from all over the United States test their cheering and tumbling skills. Some competitions are international and include teams from all over the world.

Professional football and basketball teams also have cheerleaders. They get crowds excited and on their feet. Go team!

Glossary

bases—cheerleaders who throw and catch flyers

flexible—able to stretch and move the body with ease

flyers—cheerleaders who stand on top of the bases; bases toss them into the air to perform stunts.

good sportsmanship—showing courtesy, fairness, and a positive attitude during competition

megaphones—cone-shaped devices that cheerleaders yell into; a megaphone makes a cheerleader's voice louder and directs it over a noisy crowd.

pep rallies—events held before big games to boost school spirit and encourage support of sports teams

pom-poms—balls of colorful material cheerleaders shake during their routines

rally—to stir up and encourage enthusiasm

routines—set sequences of moves performed by cheerleading squads

spotters—cheerleaders who stand by the bases during stunts; spotters are ready to catch flyers if they fall away from the bases.

squads—cheerleading teams

stunts—cheerleading moves that involve climbing, jumping, and throwing

toe touch—a jump where the legs are spread wide; the right hand reaches toward the right foot, and the left hand reaches toward the left foot.

tumble—to do a somersault, cartwheel, handstand, round-off, or handspring

To Learn More

AT THE LIBRARY
Crossingham, John. *Cheerleading in Action*. New York, N.Y.: Crabtree Pub. Co., 2003.

Gruber, Beth. *Cheerleading for Fun*. Minneapolis, Minn.: Compass Point Books, 2004.

Szwast, Ursula. *Cheerleading*. Chicago, Ill.: Heinemann Library, 2006.

ON THE WEB
Learning more about cheerleading is as easy as 1, 2, 3.

1. Go to www.factsurfer.com.

2. Enter "cheerleading" into the search box.

3. Click the "Surf" button and you will see a list of related Web sites.

With factsurfer.com, finding more information is just a click away.

Index

The images in this book are reproduced through the courtesy of: Chris Curtis, front cover; Dani Simmonds, front cover (small); James Hajjar, pp. 4-5, 8, 10, 14-15; Keystone/Getty Images, p. 6; Kristine Echica, p. 7; Yellow Dog Productions/Getty Images, p. 9; aceshot1, pp. 11, 19; Ryan McVay/ Photolibrary, pp. 12-13; Mike Orazzi/The Bristol Press, pp. 16-17; Jamie Sabau/Stringer/Getty Images, p. 18; Tina De Guzman, p. 20; Mike Roemer/AP Images, p. 21.

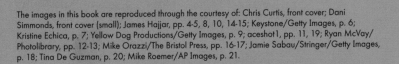